UNLOCKED

STUDY GUIDE

Copyright © 2025 by Martijn van Tilborgh

Published by AVAIL

All rights reserved. No portion of this book may be reproduced, stored in a retrieval system, or transmitted in any form or by any means—electronic, mechanical, photocopy, recording, scanning, or other—except for brief quotations in critical reviews or articles, without prior written permission of the author.

Scripture quotations marked NIV are taken from the Holy Bible, New International Version®, NIV®. Copyright © 1973, 1978, 1984, 2011 by Biblica, Inc.™ Used by permission of Zondervan. All rights reserved worldwide. www.zondervan.com. The "NIV" and "New International Version" are trademarks registered in the United States Patent and Trademark Office by Biblica, Inc.™ | Scripture quotations marked NKJV are taken from the New King James Version®. Copyright © 1982 by Thomas Nelson. Used by permission. All rights reserved. | Scripture quotations marked NLT are taken from the Holy Bible, New Living Translation, copyright © 1996, 2004, 2015 by Tyndale House Foundation. Used by permission of Tyndale House Publishers, Inc., Carol Stream, Illinois 60188. All rights reserved.

For foreign and subsidiary rights, contact the author.

Cover design by: Sara Young
Cover photo by: Andrew van Tilborgh

ISBN: 978-1-964794-73-0   1 2 3 4 5 6 7 8 9 10

Printed in the United States of America

STUDY GUIDE

UNLOCKED

MARTIJN VAN TILBORGH

CONTENTS

CHAPTER 1.	THE AMBIGUOUS GOD	6
CHAPTER 2.	BUILD *YOUR* DREAM	12
CHAPTER 3.	"THE CALL" IS NOT ENOUGH	18
CHAPTER 4.	THE ADVANTAGE FACTOR	24
CHAPTER 5.	BRAVING THE EDGE OF CHAOS	30
CHAPTER 6.	ALWAYS REMEMBER THAT YOU ARE GOD'S SECOND CHOICE!	36
CHAPTER 7.	KILLING MOSES	42
CHAPTER 8.	LONGING FOR THE WILDERNESS	48
CHAPTER 9.	THE CHALLENGE OF REAL CHANGE	54
CHAPTER 10.	LIQUID ASSETS	60
CHAPTER 11.	SUCCESS IS CLOSE AT HAND	66
CHAPTER 12.	YOU'VE GOT TALENT!	72
CHAPTER 13.	BUILDING TOWNS WITHOUT WALLS	78
CHAPTER 14.	FINDING YOUR UVP	84
CHAPTER 15.	THE DISCOMFORT ZONE	90
CHAPTER 16.	THE GREAT ATTENTION SHIFT	96
CHAPTER 17.	SHEPHERDS IN THE WILDERNESS	102
CHAPTER 18.	GENERATION NEXT	108

UNLOCKED

OPEN YOUR MIND
TO NEW POSSIBILITIES

MARTIJN VAN TILBORGH

CHAPTER 1

THE AMBIGUOUS GOD

Although God doesn't change, our perception of who He is constantly changes.

READING TIME

As you read Chapter 1: "The Ambiguous God" in *Unlocked*, review, reflect on, and respond to the text by answering the following questions.

REFLECT AND TAKE ACTION:

Moses struggled with his identity when called by God. In what ways have you questioned your own identity in moments of uncertainty? What external influences shape your understanding of who you are?

_____
_____
_____
_____
_____
_____
_____
_____

God's response to Moses's question, "Who are You?" was intentionally open-ended. How do you react when God does not give clear, specific answers? Have you ever resisted stepping forward due to uncertainty?

_____
_____
_____
_____
_____
_____
_____
_____

"And God said to Moses, 'I AM WHO I AM.' And He said, 'Thus you shall say to the children of Israel, 'I AM has sent me to you.'"

—Exodus 3:14 (NKJV)

Consider the scripture above and answer the following questions:

Why do you think God chose to identify Himself as "I AM WHO I AM" instead of giving a more specific title?

_____
_____
_____
_____
_____
_____
_____
_____
_____

In what ways has God revealed Himself to you progressively, much like He did throughout biblical history?

_____
_____
_____
_____
_____
_____
_____
_____
_____

Moses's upbringing exposed him to multiple religious influences. How has your spiritual journey been shaped by different perspectives? Have you ever had to unlearn something in order to grow in faith?

_____

_____

_____

_____

_____

_____

_____

_____

_____

_____

_____

_____

God does not change, but our perception of Him does. Can you identify a time when your understanding of God shifted? What caused that transformation?

_____
_____
_____
_____
_____
_____
_____
_____

Moses's journey required him to trust an ambiguous God. Where in your life do you need to trust God without having all the answers?

_____
_____
_____
_____
_____
_____
_____
_____

The ambiguity of God's identity suggests an invitation to an ongoing journey rather than a fixed understanding. How can you remain open to learning new aspects of who God is?

_____
_____
_____
_____
_____
_____
_____
_____

How does the way Moses encountered God in the wilderness challenge your expectations of how and where God speaks?

_____
_____
_____
_____
_____
_____
_____
_____

CHAPTER 2

BUILD *YOUR* DREAM

There is no end to the diversity of plans and purposes He has for us.

READING TIME

As you read Chapter 2: "Build *Your* Dream" in *Unlocked*, review, reflect on, and respond to the text by answering the following questions.

REFLECT AND TAKE ACTION:

There are two approaches to success: tearing others down versus building something truly great. Have you ever found yourself competing rather than creating? How can you shift your focus?

_____

_____

_____

_____

_____

_____

_____

_____

Jesus often reframed ideas of greatness, emphasizing service over status. How does this challenge common cultural notions of success?

_____

_____

_____

_____

_____

_____

_____

_____

"At that time the disciples came to Jesus and asked, 'Who, then, is the greatest in the kingdom of heaven?'"

—**Matthew 18:1 (NIV)**

Consider the scripture above and answer the following questions:

Why do you think the disciples were so preoccupied with rank and status? How do you see this mindset reflected in your own life?

_____
_____
_____
_____
_____
_____
_____
_____
_____

In what ways have you felt pressure to "prove" yourself? What did you learn from those experiences, and how does embracing God's view of greatness free you from that pressure?

_____
_____
_____
_____
_____
_____
_____
_____
_____

What fears prevent you from pursuing your dream? How does comparison with others affect your ability to move forward?

_____
_____
_____
_____
_____
_____
_____

Have you ever abandoned or downplayed a God-given dream because it didn't look like what others were doing? What would it look like to reclaim that dream?

_____
_____
_____
_____
_____
_____

What practical steps can you take to move toward building something meaningful rather than engaging in unhealthy comparison?

_____
_____
_____
_____
_____
_____
_____
_____

Reflecting on the example of Joseph and his brothers, have you ever felt threatened by someone else's success? How can you instead choose to celebrate others while still pursuing your calling?

_____
_____
_____
_____
_____
_____
_____
_____

How does knowing that God has an unlimited number of "categories" for success change your perspective on what you're called to do?

_____
_____
_____
_____
_____
_____
_____
_____

If you weren't afraid of failing, what dream would you pursue today?

_____
_____
_____
_____
_____
_____
_____
_____
_____
_____

CHAPTER 3

"THE CALL" IS NOT ENOUGH

If clarity of vision is the destination, perspective is the map itself.

READING TIME

As you read Chapter 3: "'The Call' Is Not Enough" in Unlocked, review, reflect on, and respond to the text by answering the following questions.

REFLECT AND TAKE ACTION:

Have you ever experienced a moment where you felt called by God but lacked clarity on the next steps?

_____
_____
_____
_____
_____
_____
_____
_____

John's experience in Revelation 4:1 required him to "come up higher" to gain clarity. What might you need to detach from in order to see your calling more clearly?

_____
_____
_____
_____
_____
_____
_____
_____

> *"After this I looked, and there before me was a door standing open in heaven. And the voice I had first heard speaking to me like a trumpet said, 'Come up here, and I will show you what must take place after this.'"*
>
> **—Revelation 4:1 (NIV)**

Consider the scripture above and answer the following questions:

What do you think it means to "come up here" in your own spiritual journey?

_____
_____
_____
_____
_____
_____
_____
_____

How does God's invitation to John in Revelation 4:1 challenge you to seek a broader perspective on your calling?

_____
_____
_____
_____
_____
_____
_____

Past religious templates can often shape our view of ministry. How have past experiences shaped (or limited) your expectations of God's call on your life?

_____
_____
_____
_____
_____
_____

Have you ever found yourself stuck because you were trying to follow someone else's ministry template rather than discovering your unique calling?

_____
_____
_____
_____
_____
_____

This chapter emphasizes that being called is not enough—you also need clarity, perspective, and direction. Which of these three do you struggle with the most?

_____

_____

_____

_____

_____

_____

_____

_____

Have you ever felt like you were waiting for someone else to validate your calling? How can you take responsibility for stepping into what God has placed in you?

_____

_____

_____

_____

_____

_____

_____

_____

The transition from being led to leading can be difficult. How can you embrace the responsibility of your calling rather than waiting for someone else to give you a plan?

_____
_____
_____
_____
_____
_____
_____
_____

Truly stepping into God's calling may require dismantling old mindsets. What are some limiting beliefs or past experiences you need to unlearn in order to fully embrace your purpose?

_____
_____
_____
_____
_____
_____
_____
_____

CHAPTER 4

THE ADVANTAGE FACTOR

There's no real point in trying
to keep something alive that
God has declared dead.

READING TIME

As you read Chapter 4: "The Advantage Factor" in Unlocked, review, reflect on, and respond to the text by answering the following questions.

REFLECT AND TAKE ACTION:

Describe a time when you felt like everything in your life was falling apart. Looking back, can you see how God was positioning you for something greater?

_____
_____
_____
_____
_____
_____
_____
_____

Jesus told the disciples it was to their advantage that He go away (John 16:7). Have you ever experienced a loss or a closed door that later revealed a greater purpose? What did you learn?

_____
_____
_____
_____
_____
_____
_____
_____

"But very truly I tell you, it is for your good that I am going away."

—John 16:7 (NIV)

Consider the scripture above and answer the following questions:

Why do you think Jesus described His departure as an advantage? How does this challenge the way you perceive your own losses?

_____
_____
_____
_____
_____
_____
_____
_____

If Jesus asked you to let go of something today for the sake of something greater, as He did the disciples, what would be the hardest thing for you to release, and why?

_____
_____
_____
_____
_____
_____
_____
_____

What are the "limitations" in your life right now that could actually be an advantage in disguise? How might God be using these circumstances to shift your perspective?

_____
_____
_____
_____
_____
_____
_____
_____
_____
_____
_____
_____
_____
_____
_____

Have you ever resisted a transition that was actually necessary for your growth? What happened?

___

What do you think "everything must die first" means in the context of your own calling or leadership?

___

Have you ever tried to keep something alive that God was calling you to let go of? What were the consequences?

_____
_____
_____
_____
_____
_____
_____
_____
_____

What do you think holds most people back from embracing change as an advantage? How does this apply to you?

_____
_____
_____
_____
_____
_____
_____
_____
_____

CHAPTER 5

BRAVING THE EDGE OF CHAOS

Adaptation will never make it into the history books.

READING TIME

As you read Chapter 5: "Braving the Edge of Chaos" in *Unlocked*, review, reflect on, and respond to the text by answering the following questions.

REFLECT AND TAKE ACTION:

The chapter emphasizes that true innovation happens at the edge of chaos. Can you think of a time when a chaotic or uncertain situation forced you to grow in an unexpected way?

_____
_____
_____
_____
_____
_____
_____
_____

Adaptation and optimization are not the same as innovation. How have you seen this play out in your own life, ministry, or work?

_____
_____
_____
_____
_____
_____
_____
_____

"Forget the former things; do not dwell on the past. See, I am doing a new thing! Now it springs up; do you not perceive it? I am making a way in the wilderness and streams in the wasteland."

—**Isaiah 43:18-19 (NIV)**

Consider the scripture above and answer the following questions:

What "new thing" do you feel God is trying to do in your life right now? Are you resisting it, and if so, why?

_____
_____
_____
_____
_____
_____
_____
_____

How can you position yourself to see the new thing God is doing, even when it feels like chaos?

_____
_____
_____
_____
_____
_____
_____
_____

What fears hold you back from stepping into an innovative mindset? What practical steps can you take to push past those fears?

_____
_____
_____
_____
_____
_____
_____
_____
_____
_____
_____
_____
_____
_____
_____
_____
_____

Innovation often requires discomfort. What is one area of your life where you might need to lean into discomfort in order to grow?

_____
_____
_____
_____
_____
_____
_____
_____
_____

How do you typically respond to uncertainty? Do you view it as a threat or an opportunity?

_____
_____
_____
_____
_____
_____
_____
_____
_____

What's one idea, dream, or project that you've been putting off because it feels too risky? What might happen if you embraced it despite the uncertainty?

_____
_____
_____
_____
_____
_____
_____
_____

In what ways have you settled for adaptation instead of innovation in your spiritual life or leadership?

_____
_____
_____
_____
_____
_____
_____
_____

CHAPTER 6

ALWAYS REMEMBER THAT YOU ARE GOD'S SECOND CHOICE!

God chose the people before He went to look for a messenger!

READING TIME

As you read Chapter 6: "Always Remember That You Are God's Second Choice!" in *Unlocked*, review, reflect on, and respond to the text by answering the following questions.

REFLECT AND TAKE ACTION:

The people we are called to serve come first. How does this change the way you think about your calling?

_____
_____
_____
_____
_____
_____
_____
_____

Have you ever struggled with feeling like your calling was more about you than about others? How can you shift your mindset to prioritize the people God has called you to serve?

_____
_____
_____
_____
_____
_____
_____
_____

"Then you will know the truth, and the truth will set you free."

—**John 8:32 (NKJV)**

Consider the scripture above and answer the following questions:

Our pain can become someone else's gain. What past pain in your life might God be using to help others find freedom?

_____
_____
_____
_____
_____
_____
_____
_____

If someone's breakthrough was dependent on you stepping into your calling, how would that change the urgency of your obedience?

_____
_____
_____
_____
_____
_____
_____
_____

Think of a time when you received a message or teaching that changed your life. How might God be calling you to be that voice for someone else?

_____
_____
_____
_____
_____
_____
_____
_____
_____
_____
_____
_____
_____

What do you feel is the unique message God has placed on your heart? Who needs to hear it?

_____
_____
_____
_____
_____
_____
_____
_____

Have you ever disqualified yourself from stepping into your calling because you felt inadequate? How does understanding that God equips those He calls change your perspective?

_____
_____
_____
_____
_____
_____
_____

What's one practical step you can take this week to move forward in sharing the message God has given you?

_____
_____
_____
_____
_____
_____
_____
_____

How would your life change if you truly believed that your calling was never about you in the first place?

_____
_____
_____
_____
_____
_____
_____
_____

CHAPTER 7

KILLING MOSES

God Himself puts us in situations where our status quo and "safe place" are disrupted.

READING TIME

As you read Chapter 7: "Killing Moses" in *Unlocked*, review, reflect on, and respond to the text by answering the following questions.

REFLECT AND TAKE ACTION:

In what ways have you clung to outdated leadership models, even when they no longer serve your purpose? What fears keep you from letting them go?

_____
_____
_____
_____
_____
_____
_____
_____

Moses's own journey through the wilderness prepared him to lead others. How has your personal pain or past experiences uniquely equipped you to lead others?

_____
_____
_____
_____
_____
_____
_____
_____
_____
_____

> *"Then they answered Joshua, 'Whatever you have commanded us we will do, and wherever you send us we will go. Just as we fully obeyed Moses, so we will obey you. Only may the Lord your God be with you as he was with Moses.'"*
>
> **—Joshua 1:16-17 (NIV)**

Consider the scripture above and answer the following questions:

The Israelites declared their willingness to follow Joshua, but only if God was with him as He was with Moses. How does this passage challenge you to rely on God's presence rather than past methods of leadership?

_____
_____
_____
_____
_____
_____

How does fear of the unknown impact your ability to embrace the next phase of leadership God has for you?

_____
_____
_____
_____
_____
_____
_____

Consider the statement, "Moses had to die" for the people to move forward. What leadership styles or personal mindsets must you "bury" in order to step into the future God has for you?

_____
_____
_____
_____
_____
_____
_____
_____
_____
_____
_____
_____
_____
_____
_____

We have a tendency to seek comfort in what is familiar rather than stepping into what is new. How have you seen this play out in your life or leadership?

_____
_____
_____
_____
_____
_____
_____
_____

Leadership transitions can be difficult, both personally and for those who follow. What has been your experience with major leadership shifts, and how did you navigate them?

_____
_____
_____
_____
_____
_____
_____
_____

Reflect on the statement, "God Himself disrupts our status quo." Can you identify a time when God disrupted your comfort zone to push you toward growth?

_____
_____
_____
_____
_____
_____
_____
_____

What would it look like for you to create the "mental margin" necessary to recognize and embrace new opportunities in leadership?

_____
_____
_____
_____
_____
_____
_____
_____
_____

CHAPTER 8

LONGING FOR THE WILDERNESS

More success will require more faith and more responsibility.

READING TIME

As you read Chapter 8: "Longing for the Wilderness" in *Unlocked*, review, reflect on, and respond to the text by answering the following questions.

REFLECT AND TAKE ACTION:

Success brings greater responsibility, not less. Have you ever experienced the weight of success making things harder rather than easier? Describe that experience.

_____
_____
_____
_____
_____
_____
_____
_____

Why do you think people sometimes long for "the wilderness" (a place of familiarity) instead of embracing the uncertainty of the promised land?

_____
_____
_____
_____
_____
_____
_____
_____

"The LORD had said to Abram, 'Go from your country, your people and your father's household to the land I will show you. I will make you into a great nation, and I will bless you; I will make your name great, and you will be a blessing. I will bless those who bless you, and whoever curses you I will curse; and all peoples on earth will be blessed through you.'"

—Genesis 12:1-3 (NIV)

Consider the scripture above and answer the following questions:

Have you ever struggled to believe what God says about you? What steps can you take to align your mindset with His vision for your life?

_____
_____
_____
_____
_____
_____
_____
_____

How do you currently view your abilities and your potential, and are you satisfied with your assessment? Why or why not?

_____
_____
_____
_____
_____
_____
_____

Some of the Israelites chose to settle in the wilderness rather than enter the Promised Land. How have you seen people settle for less than what God has promised?

_____
_____
_____
_____
_____
_____
_____
_____
_____
_____
_____
_____
_____
_____

Describe a time when you resisted change out of fear, only to later realize that the new season was better than what you left behind.

_____
_____
_____
_____
_____
_____
_____
_____
_____

The Israelites had to fight different battles in the Promised Land than in the wilderness. What new "battles" have you faced after stepping into a new level of leadership or faith?

_____
_____
_____
_____
_____
_____
_____
_____

What are some strategies you can use to stay strong and avoid the temptation to "go back to the wilderness" when things get difficult?

_____
_____
_____
_____
_____
_____
_____
_____

This chapter compares the wilderness to a place of predictable provision (e.g., manna every morning) but highlights that the promised land requires a different kind of faith. How do you see this principle playing out in your spiritual or professional life?

_____
_____
_____
_____
_____
_____

CHAPTER 9

THE CHALLENGE OF REAL CHANGE

The old tends to precondition our minds to keep us from the new that God wants to do now.

READING TIME

As you read Chapter 9: "The Challenge of Real Change" in *Unlocked*, review, reflect on, and respond to the text by answering the following questions.

REFLECT AND TAKE ACTION:

"Doing the right thing in the wrong season is counterproductive." Have you ever continued doing something that once worked but later led to diminishing returns? How did you recognize it was time for change?

_____
_____
_____
_____
_____
_____
_____

Continuing in old ways not only prevents future growth but eventually leads to decline. What areas of your life or ministry are at risk of decline if you don't make necessary changes?

_____
_____
_____
_____
_____
_____
_____

> *"Then we will be like all the other nations, with a king to lead us and to go out before us and fight our battles."*
>
> **—1 Samuel 8:20 (NIV)**

Consider the scripture above and answer the following questions:

Jonathan had to choose between remaining loyal to Saul's establishment outlined in Scripture or aligning himself with David, God's anointed future. In what areas of your life are you torn between tradition and transformation?

_____
_____
_____
_____
_____
_____
_____

Saul's kingship was tolerated, not initiated, by God, yet he ruled for decades. How do you discern whether something in your life or leadership is God's perfect will versus something He is merely allowing?

_____
_____
_____
_____
_____
_____
_____

When have you found yourself caught between loyalty to an old system and the courage to step into something new? What was at stake in your decision?

Jonathan recognized David's future kingship yet still died alongside Saul. Are there areas in your life where you recognize the need for change but find yourself unable to fully separate from the past?

_____
_____
_____
_____
_____
_____
_____
_____

How can you ensure that your leadership is shaped by God's voice rather than the pressures and expectations of the world around you?

_____
_____
_____
_____
_____
_____
_____
_____

What does it practically look like for you to break free from outdated structures or traditions without dishonoring what came before?

_____

_____

_____

_____

_____

_____

_____

_____

_____

What personal sacrifices might be required for you to step fully into the new thing God is calling you to?

_____

_____

_____

_____

_____

_____

_____

_____

_____

CHAPTER 10

LIQUID ASSETS

Instead of trying to separate and isolate ourselves from the tares, we need to allow ourselves to grow where we are planted.

READING TIME

As you read Chapter 10: "Liquid Assets" in *Unlocked*, review, reflect on, and respond to the text by answering the following questions.

REFLECT AND TAKE ACTION:

The concept of "liquid assets" versus "non-liquid assets" is used as a metaphor for the church's impact. How might you be unintentionally keeping your faith or leadership "non-liquid"? What practical steps can you take to ensure that the living water in your life reaches the cracks and corners of society?

_____
_____
_____
_____
_____
_____
_____

Consider a time when you tried to "bottle" or control the flow of something God was doing. What was the result? How might you approach similar situations differently now?

_____
_____
_____
_____
_____
_____
_____

"Jesus told them another parable: 'The kingdom of heaven is like a man who sowed good seed in his field. But while everyone was sleeping, his enemy came and sowed weeds among the wheat, and went away. When the wheat sprouted and formed heads, then the weeds also appeared. . . . The servants asked him, 'Do you want us to go and pull them up?' 'No,' he answered, 'because while you are pulling the weeds, you may uproot the wheat with them. Let them both grow together until the harvest.'"

—Matthew 13:24-30 (NIV)

Consider the scripture above and answer the following questions:

How does this passage challenge the way you view adversity and the presence of "weeds" in your life or ministry? What "weeds" are growing in your ministry?

_____
_____
_____
_____
_____
_____
_____

Have you ever felt tempted to act prematurely in a situation instead of waiting for God's timing? What was the result?

_____
_____
_____
_____
_____

Some of the cities with the most churches also have the highest levels of poverty and crime. Why do you think this is the case, and how can believers ensure that the presence of the church leads to transformation rather than isolation?

_____
_____
_____
_____
_____
_____
_____
_____
_____
_____
_____
_____
_____
_____
_____

Reflect on a time when you experienced God's presence in an unexpected place. What did that teach you about how He moves?

_____
_____
_____
_____
_____
_____
_____
_____

How does the metaphor of "reshaping water" apply to your personal calling? Are there areas where you need to let go of rigid expectations to allow for greater impact?

_____
_____
_____
_____
_____
_____
_____
_____
_____
_____

Not all church programs and initiatives lead to change. How can you evaluate whether your efforts are truly making a difference?

_____
_____
_____
_____
_____
_____
_____
_____

What does it mean to trust God's process even when you cannot immediately see the fruit of your labor? How does this apply to your leadership or faith journey?

_____
_____
_____
_____
_____
_____
_____
_____

CHAPTER 11

SUCCESS IS CLOSE AT HAND

It's all about what you do with what you have already got that will make the difference.

READING TIME

As you read Chapter 11: "Success Is Close at Hand" in *Unlocked*, review, reflect on, and respond to the text by answering the following questions.

REFLECT AND TAKE ACTION:

Have you ever experienced a moment where the truth of your situation was too difficult to face? How did you respond?

_____
_____
_____
_____
_____
_____
_____
_____

The widow in 2 Kings 4 found her solution within her own home. What do you already possess—skills, resources, relationships—that you may have overlooked as tools for breakthrough?

_____
_____
_____
_____
_____
_____
_____
_____

"And He said to them, 'Cast the net on the right side of the boat, and you will find some.' So they cast, and now they were not able to draw it in because of the multitude of fish."

—John 21:6 (NKJV)

Consider the scripture above and answer the following questions:

The disciples had been fishing all night without success, yet Jesus told them to cast the net on the right side. How does this moment reflect times when you've struggled despite doing everything "right"?

_____
_____
_____
_____
_____
_____
_____

Jesus's instruction required the disciples to trust and act before seeing the results. When have you had to take a step of faith without immediate evidence of success? What was the outcome? If God were to ask you the same question, how would you answer?

_____
_____
_____
_____
_____

The widow's oil only stopped flowing when she ran out of jars. What limitations in your mindset or actions might be capping the flow of God's provision in your life?

_____
_____
_____
_____
_____
_____
_____
_____
_____
_____
_____
_____

What seemingly small skill or experience in your life could be the key to your next breakthrough?

___

Reflect on a time when you were tempted to compare what you have to what others possess. What would shifting your perspective look like to help you steward what God has placed in your hands?

___

Why do you think God often uses what we already have instead of bringing in external resources?

_____
_____
_____
_____
_____
_____
_____
_____

The phrase "Success is close at hand" suggests that solutions are often within reach. What appears to be your biggest obstacle to success right now, and how does this phrase challenge your perspective of it?

_____
_____
_____
_____
_____
_____
_____
_____

CHAPTER 12

YOU'VE GOT TALENT!

The biggest tragedy happens when poverty causes someone to settle for something that is second (or third) best.

READING TIME

As you read Chapter 12: "You've Got Talent!" in *Unlocked*, review, reflect on, and respond to the text by answering the following questions.

REFLECT AND TAKE ACTION:

Poverty can be just as destructive as greed. How has your perspective on poverty shaped your decisions or fears about money?

_____
_____
_____
_____
_____
_____
_____
_____

Many people settle for jobs they hate simply to survive. Have you ever felt trapped in this way? What steps could you take to align your work with your calling?

_____
_____
_____
_____
_____
_____
_____
_____

"Give, and it will be given to you. A good measure, pressed down, shaken together and running over, will be poured into your lap."

—Luke 6:38 (NIV)

Consider the scripture above and answer the following questions:

Jesus describes a principle of abundance tied to generosity. How have you seen this principle at work in your own life or leadership?

_____
_____
_____
_____
_____
_____
_____
_____
_____

What do you think holds you back from giving? How are you currently adding value to others while you wait for your own blessing?

_____
_____
_____
_____
_____
_____
_____
_____

The "rat race" is described as a cycle that keeps people from their true purpose. What warning signs in your life indicate that you might be prioritizing survival over significance?

_____
_____
_____
_____
_____
_____
_____

If God were to evaluate how you have used your talents, what do you think He would say? Are there areas where you need to take more risks?

_____
_____
_____
_____
_____
_____
_____

A talent is both a "gift" and a "currency." How have you seen your skills translate into opportunities or resources?

_____
_____
_____
_____
_____
_____
_____
_____

Many people underestimate the potential of small beginnings. Have you ever dismissed an idea, gift, or opportunity because it seemed too small? What happened?

_____
_____
_____
_____
_____
_____
_____
_____

Financial success is a byproduct of stewarding talent well. How does this align with or challenge your current beliefs about money and faith?

_____
_____
_____
_____
_____
_____
_____
_____

Reflect on someone in your life who has stewarded their gifts exceptionally well. What can you learn from their approach?

_____
_____
_____
_____
_____
_____
_____
_____

CHAPTER 13

BUILDING TOWNS WITHOUT WALLS

Could it be that God is trying to remove the measuring lines by which we measure our work?

READING TIME

As you read Chapter 13: "Building Towns Without Walls" in *Unlocked*, review, reflect on, and respond to the text by answering the following questions.

REFLECT AND TAKE ACTION:

The man with the measuring line in Zechariah 2 had good intentions but was ultimately corrected by God. Have you ever pursued a goal with pure intentions only to realize later that it wasn't aligned with God's vision? How did you respond?

_____
_____
_____
_____
_____
_____
_____
_____

Reflect on the notion of "wall-less" cities. In what ways have you built walls to fulfill the parameters of your ministry that you established without the wisdom of God?

_____
_____
_____
_____
_____
_____
_____
_____

> *"While the angel who was speaking to me was leaving, another angel came to meet him and said to him: 'Run, tell that young man, "Jerusalem will be a city without walls because of the great number of people and animals in it. And I myself will be a wall of fire around it," declares the LORD, "and I will be its glory within it."'"*
>
> **—Zechariah 2:3-5 (NIV)**

Consider the scripture above and answer the following questions:

What does it mean for God to be a "wall of fire" around His people rather than relying on physical structures or human strategies? How have you seen this play out in your life or ministry?

_____
_____
_____
_____
_____
_____
_____

The angel corrected the man's assumption about what Jerusalem should look like. Have you ever had a moment when God disrupted your expectations about what your life or ministry should be? How did it shape your faith?

_____
_____
_____
_____
_____
_____
_____

God's Kingdom is fluid and moves with His people. How does this contrast with the way churches or ministries often function today? What are some barriers that prevent you from embracing this kind of fluidity in your own spiritual walk?

_____

_____

_____

_____

_____

_____

The man with the measuring line was an expert in his field, yet his expertise became irrelevant in the context of God's plan. Have you ever found that something you trained for or worked hard at became obsolete? How did you adapt?

_____

_____

_____

_____

_____

_____

The tendency to rely on measurable metrics can sometimes lead to legalism or limitation in faith. What is an area in your life where you need to let go of legalism or limited faith caused by self-imposed metrics?

_____
_____
_____
_____
_____
_____
_____
_____

In what ways do you see fear influencing the desire to build "walls" in your life—whether emotional, relational, or spiritual?

_____
_____
_____
_____
_____
_____
_____
_____

The image of a city without walls implies openness and vulnerability. Where in your life is God asking you to be more open, and what challenges come with that?

_____
_____
_____
_____
_____
_____
_____
_____

If God were to challenge you to expand your vision beyond what you can currently measure or control, what would that look like in practical terms?

_____
_____
_____
_____
_____
_____
_____
_____

CHAPTER 14

FINDING YOUR UVP

The devil will make you believe uniformity is a virtue, but it isn't.

READING TIME

As you read Chapter 14: "Finding Your UVP" in *Unlocked*, review, reflect on, and respond to the text by answering the following questions.

REFLECT AND TAKE ACTION:

Jesus had a clear understanding of His unique value proposition (Luke 4:18-19). What is your own God-given UVP, and how does it shape your ministry or leadership?

_____
_____
_____
_____
_____
_____
_____
_____

The temptation to copy others can be strong, especially in leadership and ministry. Have you ever struggled with trying to replicate someone else's calling rather than embracing your own? What did you learn from that experience?

_____
_____
_____
_____
_____
_____
_____
_____

> *"The Spirit of the Lord is upon me, because he has anointed me to preach the gospel to the poor; he has sent me to heal the brokenhearted, to proclaim liberty to the captives and recovery of sight to the blind, to set at liberty those who are oppressed; to proclaim the acceptable year of the Lord."*
>
> **—Luke 4:18-19 (NKJV)**

Consider the scripture above and answer the following questions:

Jesus clearly identified His mission and whom He was called to serve. If you had to write a mission statement for your own life, similar to what Jesus stated here, what would it be?

_____
_____
_____
_____
_____
_____
_____
_____

What message has God called you to share? What problem does He want you to solve?

_____
_____
_____
_____
_____
_____
_____

Jesus's message was specific and practical, not vague or abstract. How can you refine the way you communicate your purpose and calling to make it more impactful?

_____
_____
_____
_____
_____
_____
_____
_____

Many leaders struggle with answering the question, "What sets you apart?" Why do you think defining this is so difficult? How can you work toward greater clarity in your calling?

_____
_____
_____
_____
_____
_____
_____
_____

Unity does not mean uniformity. What are the defining differences between the two, and what would a balance between the two look like in an everyday scenario in your ministry?

_____
_____
_____
_____
_____
_____
_____
_____

Jesus understood who His target audience was. Have you clearly identified the people you are called to serve? How might refining your focus help you be more effective?

_____
_____
_____
_____
_____
_____
_____
_____
_____

Have you ever doubted your UVP because it seemed insignificant compared to others? How can you shift your perspective to see the value in what God has given you?

_____

_____

_____

_____

_____

_____

_____

_____

What practical steps can you take this week to embrace your UVP more fully and integrate it into your daily life and leadership?

_____

_____

_____

_____

_____

_____

_____

_____

CHAPTER 15

THE DISCOMFORT ZONE

Instead of staying relevant by copying someone else's ideas, God wants us to create relevance—to set the standard.

READING TIME

As you read Chapter 15: "The Discomfort Zone" in *Unlocked*, review, reflect on, and respond to the text by answering the following questions.

REFLECT AND TAKE ACTION:

Comfort is the enemy of growth. Where in your life have you settled for comfort instead of embracing the discomfort necessary for growth?

_____
_____
_____
_____
_____
_____
_____
_____

Leadership is a "continuous pursuit of the extraordinary in the face of the ordinary." What is an area where you feel tempted to settle for ordinary? How might it be crippling you, and what would it take for you to push beyond that?

_____
_____
_____
_____
_____
_____
_____
_____

"... to the intent that now the manifold wisdom of God might be made known by the church to the principalities and powers in the heavenly places."

—Ephesians 3:10 (NKJV)

Consider the scripture above and answer the following questions:

This passage reflects the vastness of God's creativity. What is God calling you to create, and what may be holding you back?

_____
_____
_____
_____
_____
_____
_____

In what ways have you been operating in a one-dimensional manner in your personal life and/or ministry? What would it look like to become a reflection of God's multi-dimensional nature in those areas?

_____
_____
_____
_____
_____
_____
_____

The chapter speaks about "healthy rebellion against the status quo." In what ways have you embraced or resisted this in your personal life or leadership?

_____
_____
_____
_____
_____
_____
_____
_____
_____
_____
_____
_____
_____
_____
_____

Faith is described as something that grows in tandem with pressure. Can you recall a time when increased responsibility also required increased faith? How did it shape you?

_____
_____
_____
_____
_____
_____
_____
_____

The temptation to return to "business as usual" is a pitfall for leaders. What are some warning signs that indicate you might be slipping back into old, ineffective patterns?

_____
_____
_____
_____
_____
_____
_____
_____

Reflecting on your work or ministry, in what ways do you "color outside the lines"?

When was the last time you felt truly stretched beyond your limits? What did that experience teach you about dependence on God?

CHAPTER 16

THE GREAT ATTENTION SHIFT

We need to have the courage
to challenge the very thing
that has been such a blessing
to us for so many years.

READING TIME

As you read Chapter 16: "The Great Attention Shift" in *Unlocked*, review, reflect on, and respond to the text by answering the following questions.

REFLECT AND TAKE ACTION:

Leaders often mistake busyness for effectiveness. Where in your leadership have you prioritized activity over impact? What tangible evidence can you point to that proves your efforts are making a difference?

_____
_____
_____
_____
_____
_____
_____
_____

Can you identify a time when you resorted to superficial tactics to capture attention instead of leading with authenticity? How did that impact those around you?

_____
_____
_____
_____
_____
_____
_____
_____

> *"In the days of Shamgar, son of Anath,*
> *In the days of Jael,*
> *The highways were deserted,*
> *And the travelers walked along the byways.*
> *Village life ceased, it ceased in Israel,*
> *Until I, Deborah, arose,*
> *Arose a mother in Israel. They chose new gods;*
> *Then there was war in the gates."*
>
> **—Judges 5:6-8 (NKJV)**

Consider the scripture above and answer the following questions:

The passage suggests that a nation can drift into decline through passive neglect. What aspects of your personal or spiritual life have suffered because of inattention or avoidance?

_____
_____
_____
_____
_____
_____
_____

War in the gates indicates conflict at the threshold of transformation. Have you ever faced intense resistance right before a major breakthrough? How did you respond, and what does that reveal about your resilience?

_____
_____
_____
_____

What excuses have you made for not stepping into leadership when the moment clearly called for it?

The chapter suggests that major shifts are often subtle at first. Looking back, can you identify a time when a small change—ignored or dismissed—later led to significant consequences? What can you learn from that experience?

_____
_____
_____
_____
_____
_____
_____

In what ways have you unconsciously sought validation through numbers, applause, or popularity instead of measuring success by transformation?

_____
_____
_____
_____
_____
_____
_____

Some leaders wait for a return to the past instead of moving toward the future. Are you unknowingly longing for something God has already moved beyond?

_____
_____
_____
_____
_____
_____
_____
_____

If your leadership were measured only by the eternal impact you made in others' lives, what would your legacy truly be?

_____
_____
_____
_____
_____
_____
_____
_____

CHAPTER 17

SHEPHERDS IN THE WILDERNESS

Our leadership capacity is limited to the areas where perception and truth overlap.

READING TIME

As you read Chapter 17: "Shepherds in the Wilderness" in *Unlocked*, review, reflect on, and respond to the text by answering the following questions.

REFLECT AND TAKE ACTION:

There's a difference between those who lead with vision and those who lead out of survival. Have you ever found yourself maintaining systems rather than inspiring change? What prompted that shift in your leadership?

_____
_____
_____
_____
_____
_____
_____
_____

Many leaders have a wilderness mentality that keeps them stuck. Where in your life do you feel you have settled for wandering rather than advancing, and why?

_____
_____
_____
_____
_____
_____
_____
_____

"And your sons shall be shepherds in the wilderness forty years, and bear the brunt of your infidelity, until your carcasses are consumed in the wilderness."

—Numbers 14:33 (NKJV)

Consider the scripture above and answer the following questions:

The next generation had to bear the weight of its predecessors' mistakes. What burdens are you carrying that are not yours to hold? How can you break free?

_____
_____
_____
_____
_____
_____
_____
_____

The passage shows how disbelief can delay destiny. Can you think of a time when a wilderness mindset led to unnecessary delay? Knowing what you know now, what would you have done differently?

_____
_____
_____
_____
_____
_____
_____
_____

Many leaders unknowingly reinforce a cycle of dependency rather than empowerment. Have you ever enabled complacency in those you lead by providing answers instead of equipping them to think critically?

Many leaders mistake comfort for purpose. Have you ever remained in a position, relationship, or mindset longer than you should have? What held you back?

_____
_____
_____
_____
_____
_____
_____
_____

Chaos often precedes breakthrough. How do you typically respond to uncertainty—by shrinking back or pressing forward?

_____
_____
_____
_____
_____
_____
_____
_____

The Israelites mistook the wilderness for their final destination. Is there an area in your life where you've confused transition for completion?

_____
_____
_____
_____
_____
_____
_____
_____

Leadership requires more than survival—it demands transformation. What one thing must change in your mindset for you to step up to your next level?

_____
_____
_____
_____
_____
_____
_____
_____

CHAPTER 18

GENERATION NEXT

We should invite those who raised us to be part of the new future we're creating.

There's a warning against treating the next generation as custodians rather than pioneers. Are you handing them tools for maintenance or weapons for advancement?

_____
_____
_____
_____
_____
_____
_____
_____
_____
_____
_____
_____
_____
_____
_____

This chapter challenges leaders to push the next generation forward. Have you ever withheld knowledge or opportunities out of fear of being replaced? Why?

_____
_____
_____
_____
_____
_____
_____
_____
_____

Romanticizing past successes can cost future progress. Where have you placed nostalgia above mission?

_____
_____
_____
_____
_____
_____
_____
_____
_____

What legacy are you actively building right now? If you continue leading the way you are today, what will the next generation inherit from you?

_____
_____
_____
_____
_____
_____
_____
_____
_____

The next generation will face challenges you never encountered. How can you prepare them to lead effectively in a world that is rapidly evolving?

_____
_____
_____
_____
_____
_____
_____
_____
_____

www.ingramcontent.com/pod-product-compliance
Lightning Source LLC
Chambersburg PA
CBHW062117080426
42734CB00012B/2891